France Under Louis Xv

THE WRITINGS OF
JAMES BRECK PERKINS

IN SIX VOLUMES
VOLUME IV

FRANCE UNDER LOUIS XV.

BY

JAMES BRECK PERKINS
AUTHOR OF " FRANCE UNDER THE REGENCY "

IN TWO VOLUMES
VOLUME I.

BOSTON AND NEW YORK
HOUGHTON MIFFLIN COMPANY
The Riverside Press Cambridge

DC133
.H.H

F.L 1305.33.5 (1)

✓

76✳123

TABLE OF CONTENTS.

CHAPTER I.

The Condition of France.

CHAPTER II.

THE MINISTRY OF THE DUKE OF BOURBON.

1723–1726.

CHAPTER III.

THE MINISTRY OF CARDINAL FLEURY.

1726–1743.

CHAPTER IV.

THE WAR OF THE POLISH SUCCESSION.

1733–1738.

CHAPTER V.

THE WAR OF THE AUSTRIAN SUCCESSION.

1740–1742.

CHAPTER VI.

THE EMPEROR CHARLES VII.

1742–1745.

CHAPTER VII.

RENEWAL OF THE WAR BY FREDERICK.

1744–1746.

CHAPTER VIII.

The Close of the War of the Austrian Succession.

1745–1748.

CHAPTER IX.

DUPLEIX.

1742–1754.

CHAPTER X.

THE LOSS OF AN EASTERN EMPIRE.

1754–1760.

CHAPTER XI.

THE REIGN OF MME. DE POMPADOUR.

1745–1764.

FRANCE UNDER LOUIS XV.

CHAPTER I.

THE CONDITION OF FRANCE.

AT the close of the regency of the Duke of Orleans the old régime in France was still in full vigor: the government of the country, the general social and intellectual condition of the people, were such as they long had been. Fifty-one years later, Louis XV. ended his inglorious reign; the old régime was then on the verge of dissolution, the beliefs and hopes of the French people had suffered more change than in the century preceding, the economical condition of the country had been greatly modified; a new literature had arisen, new ideas were found in books, were discussed in the salons, and were debated on the streets; the demand was widespread for new social conditions, for laws which should improve the lot of the poor, and should allow to all a greater freedom of thought and action. In this altered society the government still preserved the same outward form, but it needed no prophet to discern that institutions, which seemed as firmly rooted as those of the Medes and Persians when Louis XIV. was proclaimed the Great, were nearing their end when Louis XV. lay on his death-bed. The French Rev-

olution, like the other great events of history, sprang
from no accident or sudden caprice, — a political revolution followed an intellectual revolution.

Before relating the events of the half century, so
important in their effect on the French mind, it is
well to consider the condition of France and her
people when the death of the Duke of Orleans left
the youthful Louis XV. the ruler of that kingdom.
The government of France was an unlimited monarchy. "In my person alone is the sovereign authority," wrote Louis XV. in 1766; "legislative power
belongs to me alone; public order emanates from me;
I am its supreme guardian." It was the same language that Louis XIV. had used a century before,
and both of those monarchs correctly stated the theory
of the government of which they were the head. New
taxes could be imposed by the king and by him alone;
he could make peace and declare war; he could pronounce new laws and disregard old laws; his authority
was unchecked and unshared.

Such a form of administration would seem an absolute tyranny, as despotic as that of the Czar of Russia
or the Sultan of Morocco; but despotism in a highly
civilized state necessarily differs from despotism among
barbarous tribes or in rude forms of society.   The
actual operation of the governing power, whatever
may be its nominal form, depends upon the people
over which it is exercised.   The king of France, by
his own action and moved solely by his own desire,
could levy a tax of fifty per cent. upon the income of
his subjects; he could compel its registration by the
courts of law, and his officers could legally proceed.
with its collection; he could order the arrest of any
person, and no court had the right to review his action

or to release the prisoner; the man might remain in
confinement for forty years, with no legal means of
establishing his innocence or of obtaining his liberty;
the king could begin unjust wars, bestow undeserved
pensions, squander the proceeds of taxation on his
mistresses, and it is impossible to see where there
was redress for any grievance, except in the right of
revolution.

On the other hand, while the royal authority was
legally unrestrained, while it was liable to abuse and
was often abused, practically there were many things
which the king could not do. If he ordered a man
without trial to be taken to the Gréve and beheaded,
those who obeyed his bidding would have been liable
to no punishment. But he never gave such a com-
mand; it would have been so contrary to the recognized jurisdiction of the courts, to the ancient usages
of the kingdom, that such an act could properly be
said to be beyond his power. Innumerable privileges and local rights remained from the past, or were
founded upon bargains made between the ruler and
the ruled. Exemptions from many forms of taxation
had been granted to cities, to corporations, and to
classes; often the king failed to observe the agree-
ments made by his predecessors or by himself, but
usually these were respected. The church appealed to
its divine origin for protection against the temporal
power; the nobility possessed privileges, coming down
from the feudal period, which, though often injurious
to the community, operated as a restraint upon the un-
bridled authority of the king. The courts of justice,
though they possessed no effective veto upon his acts,
asserted their right of remonstrance, and while often
forbidden, this continued to be exercised. In a coun-

try where there was no right of petition, where political criticism was unlawful, and a reflection on the wisdom of the rulers constituted a crime, the remonstrances of the judges still furnished an opportunity for discussing the action of the government, without running the risk of a sojourn in the Bastille. Thus the French monarchy might be declared to be absolute, and yet, with equal truth, it might be said to be limited, if not by law, by customs, by privileges, by traditions, which the king had the power to disregard, but which he was sure to respect.

A just idea cannot be formed of the character of the French monarchy, nor of the probability of the king exercising wisely his great authority, without considering his modes of life, his social surroundings, the barriers of etiquette in which he was inclosed, the artificial panoply in which he was encased. Versailles, in the early part of the eighteenth century, witnessed an existence, splendid indeed, but the formality of which had stiffened into rigidity not unlike that of the courts of ancient Assyrian and Babylonian kings; if its etiquette was not so benumbing as the sombre state of Madrid, yet it did not help a monarch to understand the needs of his people, nor to perform the duties of his office.

There was, perhaps, no other person in the world who was so constantly kept in sight, whose every act was attended with such publicity, as the French king. From his rising in the morning to his retiring at night, he was surrounded by a host of attendants; he dressed and dined in public; in health and sickness, during his devotions and on his death-bed, he had about him the same multitude of courtiers. As it was their business to be smiling and respectful, so it

was his business to be smiling and affable, and neither
king nor courtier had much time left for anything
else.

Who should dress and undress him, serve him at
his table, hand him his cane, offer him his gloves,
pray for his welfare, pronounce upon him heaven's
blessing, was regulated with an anxious care. The
disputes over such questions have been preserved for
us; unimportant in themselves, they are curious as
illustrations of the customs and modes of thought of
the time. "There has been a dispute lately," writes
the Duke of Luynes, "because the officers of the
buttery pretended to the right to serve the dauphin,
when he wished to drink, to the exclusion of the
under governor; but it was decided they were wrong
in their pretension."[1] Not only did nobles contend
as to who should hand a glass of water to a child of
seven, but the clergy wrangled as to the privilege of
pronouncing grace before the king. Rather than
waive any right, occasionally all of the holy men
would be saying prayers at the same time.[2] Thus
perhaps the Lord was the better served.

Those who were received at court there spent their
lives; they listened to the sayings and watched the
countenance of the sovereign; the opportunity for a
word with him was a sufficient reward for hours of
waiting. It was not strange that this should be so.
From the favor of one man came rank, dignity, and
wealth; the ambition of the statesman for office, the
zeal of the soldier for promotion, the desire for social
prominence, the thirst for money, could all be satisfied by the monarch. "He who considers," says La
Bruyère, "that the face of the monarch causes the

[1] *Mémoires de Luynes,* i. 125.   [2] *Ib.,* i. 400.

felicity of the courtier, whose life is occupied with
the desire of seeing him and being seen by him, may
understand how the sight of God suffices for the glory
and the bliss of the saints."

The French sovereign was constantly attended by
a great number of nobles and of humbler followers;
the pomp of his court has rarely been equaled and
never excelled. All the day long an unbroken stream
of carriages rolled between Versailles and Paris.
Large as were the halls of the palace, they could
not always contain the throngs that wished to enter.
Almost every member of this multitude was a pictur-
esque object to the eye; the dresses of the gentlemen
were as rich, as varied in their material and coloring,
as those of the ladies; they were as well furnished with
laces and ruffles; the gorgeous decorations of many
orders were resplendent on the men; a profusion of
jewels set off the beauty of the women; courtesy
and grace were not often wanting in an assemblage
where almost all were of gentle birth and studied the
art of pleasing from the cradle to the grave.

A spectator has described the appearance of the
court on one evening, and the scenes which could
there be witnessed on all evenings were much the
same. The great gallery at Versailles was lighted by
three thousand wax candles, and the spectacle of the
vast hall brilliantly illuminated and filled with well-
dressed people was dazzling. There were elegant
toilettes, and many distinguished foreigners were in
attendance; one hundred and forty-two ladies were
counted in the assemblage, and the number of men
was much larger. In the centre of the gallery the
king played lansquenet; the Duke of Luxembourg
had the honor of standing behind the king's chair;

around the table were Mme. de Pompadour, the dauphin and his wife, Louis's daughters, who were still young girls, and a great number of persons, all distinguished in rank, though not all equally eminent in morality. At the further end of the room the queen had her gambling-table, at which cavagnole was played, and a number of other tables were scattered about, one presided over by the Princess of Conti, and the others by persons of less distinction. Everybody gambled, and sometimes, as was said, even at the court there were some who cheated; the queen was fond of play and she often lost; gambling-debts were among her many embarrassments. On this evening she stopped about ten, at which time supper was served, but it was not until half-past ten that Louis took his place at the lansquenet-table; at half-past eleven he and the queen retired, but the game went on.

In this great palace, to which so many had access, it was hard to keep out intruders; barriers were placed to shut off access from the salon of Hercules and the *salle des gardes*, but still, besides the well dressed who were there, others not so well dressed and without right of entrance could be seen in the assemblage. Some came for curiosity, others were attracted by the opportunities for theft that were furnished at such a place; several tobacco-boxes were stolen, and the officers in the hall made two or three arrests.

If it was difficult to exclude pickpockets from the palace, it was impossible to keep out the wind and cold. On this evening there was a good deal of wind, and some of the candles were blown out. The cold was still more annoying; at the table where the king played, by reason of the crowd gathered around, the

wind did not trouble them, but in some parts of the
gallery it was bitterly cold.[1]   Thus splendor and dis-
comfort and crime were all to be found together in
the halls of Versailles.

The most commonplace remark of the king was
caught up and repeated by the courtiers as if it were
an utterance of inspired wisdom.   One day the conversation turned on some peculiar funeral practices.
"His majesty did me the honor to say," writes the
Duke of Luynes, "'We are not subjected to such
ceremonies.'   I felt bound to reply that only his
majesty could think of such an event in his own case;
we could never even consider its possibility.   'Why
not,' said the king, 'must not this happen?'   One
cannot," adds the enthusiastic duke, moved by Louis's
admission that even he must die, — "one cannot be
too much impressed by all the marks of piety and
goodness in the king."   When Thackeray writes in
the ballad of "King Canute:" —

> "' *He* to die?' resumed the Bishop.   ' He a mortal like to us?
> Death was not for him intended, though *communis omnibus*,'"

we think this the sarcasm of the satirist, but many
a polished French courtier addressed Louis XV. in
language which differed little from that of the bishop
of King Canute.

The number of officials who surrounded the monarch was very large; he could not go from Versailles
to Marly, from the Louvre to La Muette, unless he
was accompanied by a body of attendants almost as
numerous as the Greek army at Thermopylæ.   On
the king's journey to Chantilly, says the chronicler,
there went with him over two hundred servants em-

[1] This account is given by the Duke of Luynes in his memoirs
in 1751.

ployed in the kitchen, besides sixty Swiss, whose business was to assist in serving; in all there were seven hundred persons to feed.[1] The pomp of a royal progress was not unworthy of the dignity of the monarch; trumpets sounded loudly to announce his presence; he was attended by bodies of gentlemen, proud to serve as soldiers of the king, and by companies of Swiss guards, curiously and richly dressed, and armed with weapons more gorgeous than useful, and he journeyed over the country with an amount of noise, dust, and display which could not have been exceeded by a state procession of an Assyrian or an Egyptian sovereign. It is not strange that a visit to Fontainebleau cost at least a million livres.[2] The number of persons invested with some office or charge in connection with each member of the royal family was exceeded only by the retinue of the king. More than a hundred persons were required for the care of the dauphin when he was a child of seven.[3] When Marie Leszczynski became the wife of Louis XV., over four hundred offices were at once created, to be filled by those devoted to her service, from ladies of honor to postilions and pastry cooks.[4]

The description of a single ceremonial will show the minute punctilio of this stately and formal existence. When the Princess of Lichtenstein, the wife of the Austrian ambassador, was presented to the queen, the lady of honor met her at the door, and under her escort the princess slowly advanced towards the queen,

[1] *Mém. de Luynes*, ii. 446.
[2] *Ib.*, xvii. 38.　　　　　　[3] *Ib.*, i. 62.
[4] *Dispacci Veneziani*, 213, 514, *MSS. Bib. Nat.* The list of places occupies fourteen pages of the ambassador's correspondence.

making three reverences as she went, after the last of which she paid her compliment to the queen. "In England," says our informant, "the queen salutes the wives of the ambassadors, but it is well known that this is not the usage here." In the mean time, the king having entered, every one arose. He kissed the princess on the cheek, and then she began her retreat, constantly bowing as she went, the lady of honor always at her right hand, and her face turned towards the queen, until at last the door was once more reached. Each detail was carefully watched, as its importance demanded. When the Turkish ambassador was presented, says the duke, our chronicler, and made his various reverences, "the king took off his hat either two or three times, but I could not see well enough to say which with certainty." [1]

There were members of the court who were not satisfied even with this exact and rigorous etiquette; then, as now, there were those who regretted the better manners of the past. "There is a usage which seems to be forgotten," says the Duke of Luynes; "formerly the servant of the king or queen, when entering or leaving the room, made a profound inclination, carrying the hand almost to the ground; but now I see reverences made to the queen which are no more respectful than one would make to a prime minister." [2]

The ceremonial by which the king of France was surrounded would not perhaps have smothered a powerful intellect, but it had a benumbing influence on a man of ordinary parts. So much time was required for entrées and levées, for presentations and salutations, that little remained for the work of gov-

[1] *Mém. de Luynes*, i. 376, iv. 75.
[2] *Ib.*, ii. 290.

erning a great state. It is certain that Napoleon could not have displayed his unwearied activity if he had been tied down by such an unceasing routine of ceremony. In the middle of the eighteenth century, at the beginning of an intellectual revolution, on the verge of a social revolution, this life of solemn emptiness still continued, and benumbed the intelligence of the king and of his courtiers.

Far different from the Eastern grandeur of the court of Louis XV. were the surroundings of his great rival, Frederick of Prussia. "If you want to know," writes Voltaire of Frederick, "the ceremonies of the levée, what are the *grandes* and the *petites entrées*, what are the functions of the grand chamberlain, the grand almoner, the first gentleman of the chamber, I will answer that a lackey comes to light the king's fire and shave him, that he dresses himself, and he sleeps in a trundle-bed concealed by a screen. Marcus Aurelius was not more poorly lodged." [1]

"If I were king of France," said Frederick, "my first edict would be to appoint another king, who should hold court in my place."

Louis XV. was not a man who sought relief from ceremony and adulation in any useful work; but, on the other hand, this dull grandeur was not dear to his heart; he did not derive from it the majestic satisfaction which it furnished to his predecessor. From youth to age the king was bored; he wearied of his throne, his court, and of himself; he was indifferent to all things, and unconcerned as to the weal or the woe of his people or of any living person. In his cold contempt of all mankind Louis resembled Frederick of Prussia, and, excepting the chase, there was nothing

[1] Voltaire, *Œuv. Com.*, xl. 69.

in which he took an active interest. His life was
licentious, he had many mistresses, but for none of
them did he entertain any strong affection. Mme.
de Pompadour amused him and he allowed her to
rule and ruin France as a reward, but he had for her
only a sensual and sluggish attachment; her dominion
over him was based on habit, rather than on passion.
At Versailles there was an opera on Wednesday, a
concert on Saturday, the comedy on Tuesday and Fri-
day, and gaming on Sunday, as well as on most other
days, but the king had little taste for any of these
things; he was indifferent to spectacles; even gam-
bling did not excite him.[1] He did, however, find a
lifelong pleasure in killing either bird or beast. The
history of his private life is largely the record of his
shooting. On one day we are told he killed 250 head
of game; on another he killed 100 in less than two
hours, firing 153 times.[2] Guns were less accurate
then than now, and this was a good record. In thirty
years he is said to have killed 6,400 stags, and the
number of pheasants which he bagged is beyond cal-
culation. The hunting-grounds of the French kings
were enlarged during his reign; the regulations for
the preservation of the royal game were made more
severe and onerous.

Respect and affection for the sovereign were deep
seated among the French people; these feelings had
lost none of their force at the beginning of Louis
XV.'s reign, and though they abated somewhat before
his death, yet the cries of *Vive le roi*, which always
greeted the monarch's appearance, and which we are
told by an inmate of Versailles could be heard about
the palace almost all the day long, were sincere marks

[1] *Mém. de Luynes,* i. 168.   [2] *Ib., passim.*

of popular attachment.[1] The strong affection for the sovereign which existed among the people sometimes became adulation in those attached to the person of the king. Even the priest, whose duty it was to tell the monarch of the precepts of religion and of his obligations to the King of kings, was expected to indulge in an outpouring of fulsome praise. This was called the compliment and was a recognized part of the discourse, the absence of which would have been at once noticed. It was a requirement which a loyal clergy never neglected. To take a single illustration, on Easter Day, 1742, the preacher said in his compliment to the king, "The Lord has rendered your majesty the support of kingdoms and empires, the subject of universal admiration, the beloved of his people, the delight of the court, the terror of his enemies; yet all this will but raise your great soul above what is perishable and lead you to embrace virtue and to aspire to eternal beatitude."[2] This compliment of Father Tainturin, with much more in the same strain, was, we are informed, greatly approved, and to such praise from the pulpit did Louis listen all his life. As he reflected on his personal immorality and his political insignificance, and he was quite intelligent enough to realize both, he may well have pondered upon the weight to be attached to the words of the clergy.

Naturally the splendor of the monarchy had to be paid for, and the bill was large. During the eighteenth century the condition of the national finances grew steadily worse, deficits became more alarming, bankruptcy was imminent, until the desperate condition of the treasury compelled the calling of the States Gen-

[1] *Mém. de Mme. de Campan,* i. 89.
[2] *Mém. de Luynes,* iv. 117.

eral. Had Louis XV. and Louis XVI. been able to make the ends meet, the overthrow of the old régime would not have been averted, but it would have been delayed.

What may properly be called the expenses of the monarch, the cost of the court, of palaces, of royal pleasure, royal pomp, and royal lust, were not the largest items in the expenditure of the French government, but they were very great, and a rigorous economy in them would have helped in restoring the balance between income and outgo. No reduction was attempted under Louis XV., and such an effort would have been highly distasteful to him. Of all those who had the ear of the king, there was hardly one who was not personally interested in leaving things as they were, to whom the thought of change was not distasteful and the idea of retrenchment abhorrent. The system of court life which had been fostered by Louis XIV. furnished pleasure and advantage to thousands of people, and the recipients of royal bounty wore cheerful faces, which would have been saddened by projects of reform. The innumerable offices, the inordinate expenses of the court, provided employment and gains, more or less legitimate, to almost every one with whom the king associated. The resistance of those who profited by a lavish expenditure proved too strong even for the laudable efforts of Louis XVI., stimulated by the sagacity and the resolution of Turgot, and Louis XV. was of all men the one to whom the rôle of a reformer would have been most distasteful.

Besides the great sums paid for pensions, the amount spent on the court and the royal family was not far from twenty million livres at the beginning of this

reign, and twice as much at the close, and this sum
we must multiply two or three fold to represent equiv-
alent values at the present.[1] The table of Louis XV.
and of his children cost almost four million livres
yearly, ten times the amount disbursed by a thrifty
monarch like Frederick II.[2] In every department
the expense was swollen by fraud and shiftlessness.
"What do you think this carriage cost me?" said
Louis XV. to the Duke of Choiseul. "I could buy
one like it for six thousand livres," replied the duke,
"but to your majesty, paying as a king, it should
cost eight thousand."[3] "You are far from right,"
said the king, "for it cost me thirty thousand." On
no less a scale peculation flourished in every branch
of the government; inefficiency and dishonesty went
hand in hand; an attempt to check these evils would
have been regarded as both chimerical and cruel.

The perquisites which were enjoyed by those connected with the court were often curious in their character, and were usually satisfactory in their amount.
Of many offices the duties were nominal and the legal
compensation was slight, but by recognized usage the
fortunate holders of those positions appropriated a
liberal share of the waste of the court. The ladies of
the queen's chamber were nominally paid one hundred
and fifty livres a year, but they sold for their own use
the candles which had once been lighted. This item,
which would seem insignificant, yielded to them the
very pretty sum of five thousand francs a year. So

[1] These figures are obtained approximately from the statistics
given in Forbonnais, *Recherches sur les finances.* Necker's *Compte
rendu, Maison du roi.*
[2] A Frenchman in Berlin in 1752, Voltaire, *Mém. pour servir.*
[3] *Mém. de Bezenval*, ii. 206.

great were the profits made on wax candles that a
large number of officials participated in them; the
candles unconsumed when the comedy was ended
went to the *garde-meuble*, while various persons
shared in the sale of those that remained when the
king had finished his meals. We may be sure that
the persons interested in such gains saw that the
greatest possible number of candles were lighted, and
that they were not allowed to burn too long. Every
three years the linens and the laces of the queen
were renewed in order that the lady of honor and
the royal nurse might sell the supply on hand. When
the dauphine died Mme. Brancas at once asserted
her rights to all that pertained to her toilette, which
brought no less than fifty thousand crowns; another
lady's profits on her wardrobe were eighty-two thousand livres, and in all the perquisites of various members of the court on the dauphine's death can safely
be reckoned at over a hundred thousand dollars.

The first gentleman of the chamber supplied the
king with powder and pomade, and reaped great
gains from his monopoly. The grand equerry had
the job of furnishing the Swiss guards with their uni-
forms, and his profits were larger than those of the
most fashionable tailor.

In modern days of vulgar democracy such practices
would be called plain stealing, but they were recognized by usage, and similar abuses could be found in
every branch of the French administration. It was
a gigantic system of wastefulness in which all profited,
and which no one sought to check. Even the captain
of the hunt at Fontainebleau made no less than twenty
thousand francs a year by selling rabbits; whatever
amounts were realized by the sale of the king's prop

erty, it was rarely that any of the proceeds were allowed
to find their way into the king's exchequer.[1] Indeed,
these innumerable perquisites were bestowed by a be-
nevolent monarch on courtiers who looked to him for
support, in the same way that a gentleman gives his
valet the old clothes which he would blush to sell.

The form of administration which had been per-
fected under Louis XIV. continued with little change
until the Revolution. The chief authority was in the
hands of secretaries of state, to each of whom was
assigned an amount of work which required for its
performance the greatest industry and the highest
ability. The choice of the ministers was determined
by the intrigues of the court and the caprice of the
monarch, and, as a result, few men of capacity filled
these positions during the eighteenth century. While
Fleury was prime minister he exercised a certain
supervision over his associates, but after his death
unity of purpose was rarely found among the advisers
of the king. As a rule, each secretary was jealous of
his companions; his chief anxiety was lest any of them
should obtain in large degree the confidence and favor
of the sovereign. The man fortunate enough to be
chosen as secretary was admitted to the intimacy of
the king, he could enrich himself and his friends, he
was the object of envy to his fellows; dismissal from
office was the manifest mark of royal disapproval, a
disgrace which few had sufficient philosophy to bear
with equanimity. The minister was in little danger
of overthrow from any public disfavor; whether he
was loved or hated by his fellow citizens was not
likely in any way to affect his tenure of office. But

[1] *Mém. de Luynes,* ii. 369; iii. 300; vii. 383 *et pas.;* Taine,
L'Ancien Régime, 87.

he was exposed to dangers of a different nature: the
complaints of those who had the opportunity of whis-
pering their discontent to the monarch when he was
putting on his shirt or taking off his boots; the insinu-
ations of his companions at the supper-table; most
dangerous of all the ill will of her who, for the time
being, possessed the royal affections, might any day
bring the dreaded order to turn over the seals of office
and retire to his château in the provinces.   Naturally,
therefore, the secretary sought to make friends of
members of the court, to advise no measure which
would interfere with their privileges, to oppose no
act of benevolence which they might request from the
king.   Still more was it for his interest to enjoy the
favor of the mistress, to assist her in every demand
for money or rank, to consult her in the distribution
of patronage, to ask her advice as to the policy of the
state.   The shameful influence exerted by the mistresses of Louis XV. in the government of France is
the chief scandal of his reign, and had much to do with
undermining the monarchical traditions of the French
people.   Men were made ministers of state because
they could turn off a neat rhyme on the favorite's
charms, and men were dismissed from office because
they dared to oppose her wishes.

So firmly was the power of such women established
under Louis XV. that it seemed an integral part of
the system of government; in nations where this was
not found, courtiers recognized a defect in the constitution.   The young Count of Gisors, son of Marshal Belle Isle, visited England in 1754.   It was
not strange that he should have thought St. James
hideous and the English court small and sombre when
compared with that of Versailles, but another differ-

ence attracted his attention as he considered the relative positions of Mme. de Pompadour and the Countess of Yarmouth. "In every other monarchy," he writes, "the mistress of the king shares his power; here she only shares his impotence."[1]

Even though no woman's whim interfered, Louis was prone to make a capricious choice of his servants. His indolent and selfish nature was affected by trifles; though he was indifferent to the abilities of his ministers, he was critical as to their manners: he never recalled Chauvelin to his councils because his jokes, his familiarity, and his loud laughter were distasteful; he dismissed Amelot, the secretary for foreign affairs, because he could not endure his perpetual stuttering.[2]

The administration in France was highly centralized, and to superintendents was assigned the duty of regulating the affairs of the provinces in accordance with the principles adopted at Versailles. The extensive power vested in these officers has been an object of denunciation from Richelieu's day to ours, but as a whole it was probably in furtherance of good government. Certainly the power exercised by them was very large. "The kingdom of France," said Law, "is governed by thirty superintendents, and on them depends the misery or happiness of the provinces, their abundance or their sterility." Hardly an object of human interest was without their jurisdiction; the administration of justice, the finances of the city, the highways of the town, the apportionment of taxation, the dispersion of Huguenot assemblies, alike required the attention of the all-pervading superintendent. His

[1] *Journal of Count of Gisors,* February–April, 1754; cited by Rousset, *Vie du Comte de Gisors.*

[2] *Mém. d'Argenson,* ix. 58, 64.

action could be overruled by the authorities at Versailles, but little of this mass of detail found its way to the notice of a secretary whose mind was too closely fixed on the court to give much thought to the condition of the provinces.

Power as extensive as this was often abused; there were superintendents who were bigoted and inefficient and corrupt; but, on the whole, their work seems to have been as well done as was possible with any system that was then practicable. Many of the duties imposed upon them might wisely have been intrusted to local bodies, but in the political condition of France at that period an intelligent and effective system of local government was impossible, unless accompanied by a degree of political freedom which would at once have put an end to the old régime. The superintendents were always active and usually intelligent, and the extensive power vested in officials who were themselves dependent on the central government helped to unify the French people.

The administrations of such men as Aguesseau in Languedoc and Turgot at Limoges were long remembered for the benefits they wrought in the districts under their charge.

The influence of the city governments and of other local bodies was not sufficiently important to require any detailed notice. By various means they had been deprived of any independent power: the appointment of officials was largely in the hands of the king; their duties were nominal; the people had little voice in their selection, and little concern as to their conduct. In the early part of the eighteenth century there was no other section of the world where the theory of local government was so admirably developed as in New

England; there was no civilized country in which it was more torpid and unimportant than in the greater portion of France, and this fact alone will go far to account for the differences between the revolutions of 1776 and 1789.[1] In Languedoc, Brittany, and a few other districts, the ancient provincial states had escaped annihilation, but their power to regulate the amount contributed to the general government by those they represented, which had once been important, was now hardly more than a registration of the royal will. The provincial states, like the governors of the provinces, had the form of power, but not the reality. They might have furnished a nucleus for the development of legislative bodies, somewhat akin to the legislatures of the American States, but the tendency of political change in France was not in that direction; in the discussions of the eighteenth century there was little demand for any local subdivision of political action; the most ardent republican of the Convention was as eager an advocate of centralization as Richelieu or Louis XIV.; the provincial states, which were feeble at the beginning of the eighteenth century, passed out of existence at the close of it.

During the reign of Louis XV. the only check upon the authority of the king was found, not in any representative assemblage which could assert a right based on past tradition or on present expediency, but in the judicial bodies whose claim to exercise legislative action had little foundation in the past and was of little value in the present. The nobility of the robe

---

[1] For a somewhat fuller statement of the condition of the local bodies in France under Louis XIV., which was little changed under Louis XV., I would refer to *France under the Regency*, p. 304 *et seq.*

enjoyed privileges hardly inferior to those of the nobility of the sword; it was no better fitted to render
important political service to the state. It is not
strange, therefore, that the constant quarrels between
the Parliament of Paris and Louis XV. served no
useful purpose. A royal edict, in order to be enforced,
had to be registered with the courts, but if this registration was refused, the king in his own person could
hold a bed of justice and compel it. It is manifest,
therefore, that though the parliament might remon-
strate with the sovereign, it could not control his
action; it could delay the registration of an edict, but
it could not prevent it. Nor from the constitution of
the body was it possible that it should ever become a
fit organ for the expression of the popular will. We
shall have occasion to relate frequent contests between
the king and the courts during the reign of Louis
XV. The cause espoused by the judges was usually
popular with the people. But when later in the century there came a demand for popular institutions,
and the overthrow of the privileges which formed so
large a part of the old régime, it is not strange that
the judges were soon arrayed in opposition to changes
which would be fatal to their own position in the community. The growth of the French parliaments is
interesting as a chapter in legal history, but it is not
important as a part of the constitutional history of the
French kingdom.

In considering the condition of France at the beginning of Louis XV.'s reign it is proper to give special attention to the position of the nobility, for politi-
cally as well as socially its influence was far greater
than that of either the church or the third estate.

The French nobility was a large body; new mem-

bers were constantly added, and its limits were vaguely
defined; it is difficult, therefore, to say with accuracy
in what measure the administration of the country
remained in its hands. It was the policy of Louis
XIV. to restrict the influence of the great nobles,
whose families traced their origin far back in French
history, and whose ancestors had once ruled provinces almost as independent sovereigns. Secretaries
of state were more often chosen from officials connected with the parliament, or from superintendents
who had shown ability, than from nobles who bore
names like those of Condé, or Rohan, or Bouillon. In
this, as in every tradition of government, Louis XV.
sought to follow in the footsteps of his ancestor.
There were no families in France during the eighteenth
century exercising a political influence to be compared with that of the Bedfords, or the Pelhams, or
the Newcastles in England. But illustrious houses
like the Condés or the Bouillons formed a small part
of the French aristocracy. The parliamentary families should not be regarded as part of the third
estate; they were not improperly called the nobility of
the robe, inferior indeed to that of the sword, but
still identified in interest with the aristocracy, rather
than with the commonalty of France. Men who had
sprung from modest origins, but had obtained the
prizes of the state, became founders of new families,
equal in wealth and in rank to those of more ancient
lineage; the descendants of Colbert and Fouquet and
Louvois mingled on no very unequal terms with the
descendants of nobles who had conquered at Bouvines,
or been defeated at Agincourt. Admitted into a privileged body, enjoying the rank, the titles, the immu-
nities of an aristocracy, naturally they espoused its

interests and shared its prejudices. Centuries are not required to instill into the blood a lively conception of the difference between nobleman and commoner. The father of the famous Duke of St. Simon was a poor country gentleman elevated to the peerage by the caprice of his master, but his son could have been no more deeply imbued with aristocratic prejudices if he had traced his rank to Hugh Capet instead of to Louis XIII.

We can justly say that the administration of France under Louis XV. was largely in the hands of the aristocracy, and certainly the traditions of that body had a controlling influence on the policy of the country. Even though a secretary of state might belong to a parliamentary family, or came from still humbler stock, the courtiers, the officers of the army, those attached to the person of the king, belonged with few exceptions to the order of the nobility.

At this period nearly two hundred thousand persons formed the second estate, as the nobility was officially called; they were but one per cent. of the population of France, but they received a larger amount of consideration from the government and from the world than the other ninety-nine parts. To most readers of French history its interest still centres in the vision of a magnificent monarch, attended by dukes and marquises, resplendent in powdered hair, embroidered coats, and jeweled swords, and by ladies who were always charming, often beautiful, and sometimes virtuous. It is not a complete and a philosophical conception of the history of a great people, but it would be idle to disregard the importance of the court life under the old régime.

There was, however, a large class of the nobility

who were not found among the gorgeous butterflies
that adorned Versailles; gentlemen who could show
the quarterings necessary for entrance to any noble
order, but who knew as little of Paris as many an
English squire knew of London. These country
gentry for the most part were reduced in fortune, and
exercised a small influence in their districts. The
want of money, the lack of some powerful friend who
could procure for them a position at court, were generally the causes which kept them at home. Trade
was forbidden, the practical qualities by which estates
are made more valuable were not common among
them, and the fortunes of many gentle families steadily decreased. Each son inherited the privileges and
the traditions of his order, but his material inherit-
ance was often sadly inadequate for the support of a
gentleman, who could find no way of bettering his
fortunes without derogating from his rank. He became "the high and mighty seigneur of a dovecot, a
frog-pond, and a warren." A superintendent tells us
that in his district, out of thousands of gentle birth,
there were not thirteen who had incomes of twenty
thousand francs. Scorning any occupation but the
chase, they blushed to work and died of hunger.[1]

Thus reduced in fortune, they led a cramped and
useless existence. The French gentlemen as a class
took little part in the affairs of the community; few
of them bore any resemblance to the country gentry
who exerted so great and so beneficial an influence in
England. They were indeed less apt to get fuddled
drinking with the farmers at the tavern, but neither
had they any taste for the useful work of the Quarter
Sessions, nor that active and hearty coöperation in

[1] Rétif de la Bretonne, *La vie de mon père*, i. 146.

matters of local interest which make the squire the
chief figure, and usually a popular figure, in every
English hamlet.

The gentlemen who were debarred from the bril-
liant existence of the court cherished in no less degree
the pride of their order. The duke who stood by the
king at his dinner and was admitted into his bed-
chamber was no more tenacious of the deference due
his rank than the country gentleman who lived in a
dilapidated château on poorer fare than many a skilled
mechanic, and who wandered over his scanty acres
with a hungry dog at his heels and a rusty sword at
his side. Voltaire was made a gentleman of the
king's chamber, and the Chevalier de l'Huillière ex-
pressed the sentiments of his class when he wrote, " I
am informed that the king has bestowed the office of
gentleman of his chamber upon one Arouet, known as
Voltaire. The king will not affront the nobility by
releasing this fellow from furnishing proofs of his
gentle birth, which he could only find on his mother's
side, for on his father's he is a roturier. To do
this would dishonor gentlemen of name, who have
been noble from father to son from time immemo-
rial."[1] The orthography and the grammar of this
letter are lamentable, and those who were outraged
that an office should be bestowed on one who could
not show his sixteen quarterings were often as ignorant as they were proud. Even in 1789, in the
cahiers prepared for the States General, we find numerous requests from country gentlemen for some
mark—a cross or a ribbon—which should proclaim
to the world that its wearers were of noble birth.[2]

---

[1] Fillon, *Lettres inédites de la Vendée*, 116, 7.
[2] Taine, *L'Ancien Régime*, 48.

Undoubtedly there were exceptions; there were nobles, like the father of the great Mirabeau, who were in no way connected with the court, and whose careers were active and useful. At the beginning of the Revolution the peasants of the Vendée remained constant to the principles espoused by the upper classes, and their devotion proves that in this district the gentlemen still retained their position as leaders of the community. Such cases were exceptional; as a rule, the provincial nobility were encased in a stupid pride, which kept them aloof from their neighbors of less degree; they showed no capacity for useful work or for any work; they possessed no hold over a community which they neither guided nor aided.[1]

If the life of some gentleman whom scanty fortune condemned to vegetate in the provinces was barren and dull, it was far otherwise with the great nobles. To an uncommon degree they had within their reach the objects of human desire; they possessed rank and wealth; they were free from the cares and necessities which cramp the existence of most; they received great benefits from the state, and were exempt from most of its burdens. Few lots would seem more enviable than that of the head of a great French family during the eighteenth century, living in a country which attracted the attention and excited the admiration of all Europe, forming part of a magnificent court, where the splendor of the king and the greatness of the country furnished innumerable opportunities for the acquisition of dignity and power and wealth.

---

[1] "Les seigneurs," said the Marquis of Mirabeau, speaking of the rest of the population, "ne leur sont plus bons à rien ; il est tout simple qu'ils en soient oubliés comme ils les oublient."

Such an aristocracy naturally dazzled and delighted all beholders. The training of its members from childhood fitted them for intercourse with their fellows; they had tact and polish and good breeding. A lad of twelve could turn a neat compliment to a guest; a girl was drilled each hour of the day in the minutiæ of etiquette. " Be careful not to disturb your rouge, and not to tear your robe, and not to disarrange your headdress, and then amuse yourself," said a mother to a young girl going to a children's party.[1] They were drilled for a life of social display; the marquis of ten, in powdered hair and with a sword at his side, walked with as much dignity as the duke his father; his sister of twelve was versed in the use of the rouge-pot, and submitted herself to the arts of the hair-dresser with as resigned a grace as the duchess her mother. If a nobleman often grew up knowing very little else, at least he was taught good manners, and for the career before him this was by far the most useful accomplishment which he could acquire.

The social life of the nobility and the changes which the century produced will be discussed later. It is rather as a political element in the body politic that they will here be considered, and we are first impressed by the amount which they cost the state. Alike the feudal dues which remained as a relic of the feudal power vested in the nobility of a former age, and the heavy burden which their successors imposed upon the national treasury, increased the weight of taxation, and were a serious check upon the prosperity of the larger portion of the community.

Life at Versailles was costly, even though the king defrayed many of the expenses of those whom he

---

[1] Cited by Goncourt, *La femme au* 18ᵉ *siècle.*

regarded as his guests. The establishments of the great nobles were on a colossal scale, the servants were numerous, the cost of entertainment was large, and necessary expenses were swollen by shiftlessness. As a result, the nobility as a body were involved in debt; even though the revenues from their estates were swollen by pensions and emoluments received from the king, a large proportion were in a chronic state of insolvency. The Duke of St. Simon had an income of almost eighteen hundred thousand livres, yet his creditors had to be content with fifty cents on a dollar of their claims; Marshal Estrées left two million livres of debts; at twenty-six the Duke of Lauzun was already two millions in debt; M. de Chenonceaux lost seven hundred thousand francs at play in a single night. The Duke of Bourbon had an income of two million livres, and owed six millions when he died.[1] The country gentlemen were embarrassed because their receipts were so small, and the great nobles were bankrupt because their expenditures were so large.

Rarely did a nobleman give any attention to improving the value of his property, and to engage in business enterprises was unknown. Arthur Young said he could generally distinguish the estates of great nobles by their bad condition. " Whenever you stumble on a grand seigneur you are sure to find his property a desert." " I will wager," said a stranger, "that this inclosure belongs to the seigneur." " It does," replied the peasant. " I thought so," continued the traveler, " when I saw it was covered with briers and thorns." [2] The dilapidation of fortunes was sometimes repaired by marriages with the daughters of

[1] *Mém. de Luynes*, iii. 123 ; iv. 445 *et pas.*
[2] Mirabeau, *Traité de la population*, i. 42.

bankers or government contractors, but such alliances
were not as common as they are now, and the tendency of an extravagant class was to become an embarrassed class.   Yet whatever was the condition of
the hereditary estates, though rents were falling and
mortgages were growing, a man of the world, as has
been truly said, expected that there should be money
in his pocket, a fine coat in his dressing-room, powdered valets in his antechamber, a gilded carriage
standing at his door, and a choice dinner served upon
his table.[1] In certain directions he was willing to
disquiet himself in order to obtain the means for such
an outlay, but the only source of supply to which he
could resort was the liberality of the king and the
treasury of the nation.

If a nobleman was in favor at court and was in
financial distress, — and the two things frequently went
together, — it was to the king that he turned for relief,
nor was the prayer for aid often refused.   The Prince
of Conti was given a million and a half livres to pay
his debts ; the Countess of Polignac had four hundred
thousand for the same purpose, and the list of similar
benefactions would be endless.

If assistance was not granted directly from the
treasury, it was often furnished by expedients for
which the public at last had to pay.   As the Prince
of Carignan was in straits, he was allowed to keep a
gambling-house in Paris, with the profits of which he
might repair the waste of his fortune.

The Duke of Luynes tells us of the efforts of a
person who wished to share in the profits made from
the farm of taxes.   At first he promised M. de la
Trémoille fifty thousand crowns to secure him the

---

[1] Taine, *L'Ancien Régime*, 165.

position, but for some reason this negotiation fell
through. At last he was promised the place upon condition of paying forty thousand crowns, with which
to discharge a gambling-debt of the Duke of Richelieu.[1] It was necessary that the profits to be derived
from the position should be sufficient to defray the
bribes required to obtain it, and so they were. Each
one of the associates connected with the farms received
annually the sum of two hundred and fifty thousand
livres, and in addition the gains of the association
during one term of nine years were figured at fifty-four
millions.[2]

The demands of the nobility for pecuniary aid were
regarded as well founded; alike privileges and pensions and exemptions from taxation were based upon
a claim of right, upon services rendered in the past
for the support and defense of the monarchy, and
which were supposed still to be rendered in the present. In the service of the king the members of the
second estate, it was said, were ready to shed their
blood; in times of peace they were his counselors,
and in the advice of noblemen possessing the advantage of leisure, and raised above need, a wisdom and
disinterestedness could be found not to be expected
from those born to a humbler lot. It was just, therefore, that offices of profit and responsibility should be
intrusted to those who were entitled to their gains and
fitted for their duties. Such was the theory of the
advantages of an aristocracy as a governing class, and
it is necessary to study the history of France in the
eighteenth century to see how far this conception was
justified.

The embarrassed condition of the national finances

---

[1] *Mém. de Luynes*, ii. 61. [2] *Ib.*, x. 166.

which was chronic under Louis XV. was not altogether due to excessive expenditure. Certainly there
was great opportunity for retrenchment, yet the expenses of the government under the old régime were
not greater than the country was able to bear; it is
doubtful whether the monarchical establishment was
any more costly than the democratic institutions by
which it has been succeeded. Wars were more frequent in the last century than in this, but while they
lasted longer they cost less, and the expense of the
army in times of peace was small in comparison with
the sums now expended by most European nations.
Twenty million livres a year would perhaps represent
the sums annually paid in pensions to the aristocracy.
In addition to this there were the excessive amounts
allowed to the holders of many offices; the Governor
of Languedoc had a salary of one hundred and sixty
thousand livres, the Governor of Burgundy received
one hundred thousand, the position of grand master
was worth as much; the list of lucrative offices was
a long one. The amount spent upon the royal family
was a yet more serious item. Aside from the civil list
proper, the expenses of the monarch himself, were the
increasing sums expended upon members of his family.
While Louis XV.'s daughters were still little more
than children, it was said that each of them cost the
state a million annually, and a few years later the
two brothers of Louis XVI. succeeded in squandering
every year eight millions of the public moneys.

Such extravagance can justly be condemned, yet it
is equaled by the salaries of an excessive number of
minor officials in the present French government, and
it is far exceeded by the pension list of the United
States. It may, indeed, be said that the sums thus

expended in our own day benefit large numbers, while those paid out under the old régime profited only a small class; yet considered as a burden upon the national wealth, it is questionable if the cost of government absorbed any larger proportion of the resources of the governed.

It was not the amount taken by taxation so much as the apportionment of taxation which rendered its burden almost unbearable. If the condition of the lower classes was bad, and the finances of the government were involved, the explanation is to be found chiefly in the exemptions granted the privileged classes. The number of those who profited by such abuses was constantly increasing, and thus a larger proportion of the national wealth was withdrawn from its just burden of taxation. A courtier of Louis XIV. said that whenever his majesty created an office, the Lord created a fool who would purchase it. The purchaser was by no means a fool; the salaries allowed the holders of the countless useless offices created at this period usually amounted to at least a reasonable interest on the sum paid for the place, and the other advantages which resulted were often far more valuable than the yearly stipend received from the treasury. There were thousands of positions which secured to their holders a large degree of exemption from the burdens of taxation. The position of some petty civic official or of some useless court functionary might not seem specially enviable, but if it conferred upon him the rank of nobility, and thereby secured relief from the ordinary burdens of the state, the advantage to the incumbent was large, and in every case it was purchased at the expense of other taxpayers.

The nobility were by no means exempt from all forms of taxation, but where the law did not spare them altogether their social position secured a large degree of immunity. The Duke of Orleans said he saved three hundred thousand livres every year because the taxing officers grossly underestimated his property; the princes of the blood did not pay one twelfth of the amount for which they were justly liable; on an average, the assessment on the estates of gentlemen was probably not over one sixth of the sum which would have been levied on property of the same value in the hands of roturiers.[1]

At the beginning of Louis XV.'s reign the bourgeoisie filled a less important place than at its close. With the development of commerce resulted a growth of wealth which secured for its possessors an increasing influence in society and the state. Many of the fortunes accumulated would be regarded as considerable even in our days. Samuel Bernard, the great banker, was said to have left thirty millions; M. de Bellegarde, a farmer of taxes, had a fortune of eight millions, and the list of those whose wealth was reckoned by millions was not a small one. By the very fact of their riches such men were brought into intimate relations with the aristocracy, whose society they sought, and whose vices they imitated more easily than their virtues.

Bernard led a life of magnificent display; his table alone cost him one hundred and fifty thousand livres a year; his mistress was given a great estate; his sons squandered fortunes; his daughter married the Marquis of Mirepoix. Some blamed the marquis, writes a

[1] The evils resulting from an under-assessment of the property of nobles are often referred to by Turgot.

contemporary, for allying himself with a family so lacking in lustre, but he adds, "in these days nothing but money is considered." [1] Even in the courtly era of Louis XIV., Madame de Sévigné had written that the millions were always of good family. The lives of many of these parvenus, the most of whom gained their wealth in transactions with the state, were too often a poor reproduction of the reckless career of spendthrift nobles. Madame d'Epinay has described the routine of existence at her husband's, a man who, like many of his fellows, combined educated and artistic tastes with every folly of conduct. When he arose his valet hastened to assist in the toilette, two lackeys were on hand to receive his orders, and a secretary to attend to his correspondence. Then followed what seems a burlesque on the scenes which attended the king's rising: M. d'Epinay walked into his antechamber amid two rows of parasites and protégés, dealers and merchants, lackeys and beggars, and, alas! always a goodly assemblage of creditors, who danced attendance long before they were able to obtain their pay.[2] His father acquired wealth as a farmer of taxes, and the son inherited a fortune, and an office of which the gains were as large as they were unconscionable. No riches could keep pace with his prodigality, and he squandered his money on every device that could be suggested by dissipation and improvidence. With all this he was a polished and an agreeable man. He had a smattering of every useless accomplishment; he was a fair musician, and a bit of a poet; he had a taste for architecture and painting and cooking, and was a reasonably good carpenter; he

[1] *Journal de Barbier*, August, 1733.
[2] *Mém. Mme. d'Epinay*, 307.

ruined himself and his family with the utmost amiability. His relations with his wife are a curious and
a melancholy picture of the social condition of the
time, for he consulted her with frankness as to appro-
priate gifts for the actresses on whom he squandered
countless thousands. At last his dissipation cost him
his office, as it had exhausted his fortune; separated
from his family, ruined in position, hopelessly bankrupt, he hummed and thrummed through life to the
end, giving dainty little suppers, patronizing the stage,
adoring actresses, with perfect affability, courtesy, and
contentment.

It was not by such men that society could be changed
for the better, yet as years went on the upper middle
class assumed greater importance; the influence of
commerce and literature became larger, while that of
Versailles grew less. Before Louis's reign was ended,
the public sought inspiration from houses at Paris
where gathered philosophers and economists, rather
than from the salons of an ancient aristocracy. But
in the early part of the century the middle classes
exerted little influence in the administration of the
state.

To the most important class in the population the
government gave least attention; upon the tillers of
the soil the burden of taxation fell most heavily, and
little heed was given to the amelioration of their lot.
Yet no one can understand the course of French history without giving to the character of the French
peasantry more study than it has often received.
Among the national characteristics of the French, as
they are generally conceived, are wit, frivolity, fickle-
ness, a readiness for political change. The French
peasants have few of the qualities which are assumed

to be those of the whole nation; they have been conservative, unwilling to deviate from the usages of the
past, slow to adapt themselves to the needs of the
future, untiring in their industry, often narrow in
their intelligence, yet fond of gain, and eager to add
sou by sou to their savings, and acre by acre to their
little parcels of land. Among them neither wit nor
intellectual brightness has found a fertile soil, but
they have contributed to the nation's character a certain stubborn tenacity, for which it has not always
received credit. It is from the innumerable petty
hoards of a thrifty and often an avaricious peasantry
that the money has been forthcoming which has saved
France from financial ruin in the worst crises of her
history. The country depends on a class whose strong-
est quality is an indomitable persistence, and this has
enabled the French people to escape the overthrow
with which they have so often been threatened.

The contrast between the upper classes and the
peasantry in France has always been far more marked
than between the corresponding orders in England.
Broad as are the distinctions that result from differences in birth and education and wealth, yet there has
always been much in common between an English
nobleman and an English yeoman; through all the
centuries of English history it is easy to see the characteristics which have bound together the estates of
the realm. It has not been so in France; either in
the eighteenth century or the centuries prior it is hard
to find any point of resemblance between the peasant
who labored in the fields and the gentleman who lived
in the château. There was no such difference in
character and tendencies and tastes between the peer
and the plowman in England as that which in France

seemed to draw an impassable line between Monsieur le Marquis and Jacques Bonhomme.

At the present time, one half of the population of France is occupied with the culture of the soil; the proportion was somewhat larger in the last century, and under Louis XV., of twenty million people, nearly fifteen millions belonged to the peasantry.[1] Not only were they the largest class, but they were by far the largest contributors to the national wealth. Even now the wealth of France is chiefly agricultural, and a century and a half ago French manufactories were comparatively small and the era of great industrial development had not begun. The French as a people have not been preëminent in commercial intelligence; they do not equal the English in business enterprise; they have had poor success in colonial development; the nation owes its prosperity chiefly to the unremitting toil given to a fertile soil, and to the unwearying thrift by which the small but steady gains of agriculture have been accumulated until they reached enormous proportions. The soil of France is rich, but in the culture of it more has been due to the indefatigable industry of the peasants than to the intelligence they displayed in their methods. More than a century before, Olivier de Serres, the most famous of French agricultural writers, had bidden his countrymen to cling to the plow of their ancestors, and to beware of innovations.[2]

---

[1] In 1792, Arthur Young estimated the urban population at six millions and the country population at twenty millions. *Travels in France*, 353. The latter has changed little in a century, being still about nineteen millions; the increase has been entirely in the cities.

[2] *Théâtre d'Agriculture.*

No advice was less needed. The French people
do not take readily to economical novelties, nor have
farmers in any nation been prompt to change the
modes of culture which they learned from their sires,
and the peasants have been the most conservative
among Frenchmen, and the most averse to change
among farmers. Arthur Young commented repeat-
edly on the backward condition of French agriculture.
In Brittany, he said, husbandry had not further advanced than among the Hurons.[1]

In some districts the conditions were better, for the
differences in intelligence and prosperity in different
parts of the country were far greater than they are
now. Yet if a peasant who lived in the days of
Charlemagne could have revisited the scene of his
labors in the early part of Louis XV.'s reign, he
would have seen few notable changes in the manner
in which the soil was cultivated; the great forests had
somewhat diminished, the amount of improved land
had increased with an increasing population, but he
would have found his descendants plowing and plant-
ing and reaping in much the same way that he did
himself.

Imperfect as were the means adopted, the results
were large. Working with the poorest tools and,
from the conservatism of his nature, slow to apply
improved methods, even if he had been aware of their
existence, yet by rising early and laboring late the
peasant made his little piece of land yield a large
increase.

In great measure this was due to the fact that he
was working for himself and not for another. Peasant
proprietorship in France is far from being a new

[1] *Travels in France*, 123.

thing, and the extent of it furnishes some criterion of
the prosperity of different periods. A considerable
portion of the soil belonged to peasant owners as far
back as the thirteenth century, and complaints were
frequent of the extent to which the land was subdi-
vided. At the time of the Revolution, Arthur Young
thought that over one half of the soil was in the pos-
session of small proprietors. This estimate was too
high. About one third of French soil is now owned
by the peasantry, that is, by men whose holdings are
less than twenty acres, and over three million five
hundred thousand proprietors cultivate their own
land.[1] There has been some increase in peasant proprietorship since the downfall of the old régime,
although this has been less than is supposed; in the
early half of the eighteenth century, the peasantry
undoubtedly owned one fifth of all the soil of France,
and they owned more than one fifth of that which was
actually cultivated.[2] The great forests, the vast tracts
of waste land, belonged to the government or to large
owners, and probably almost one third of the land on
which crops were raised was property of the men who
tilled it.[3] The wealth drawn from the soil was vastly
increased by the number of small proprietors. A contemporary, who was himself a nobleman, estimated
that on an average the land owned by the peasantry
was four times as productive as that owned by the
nobility.[4] " The magic of property turns sand to

[1] *Enquête agricole*, 1882.

[2] Lavergne, *Economie rurale*, 49.

[3] The Vicomte d'Avenel, in his *Histoire économique*, thinks
that the subdivision of land in 1789 was about the same propor-
tionally as at present, but the amount under cultivation is now
much larger. (Page 287.)

[4] Argenson, *Considérations sur le gouvernement de France.*

gold," Young wrote, as he saw the comfortable little houses standing on the sandy soil of French Flanders.

Yet the result of unremitting toil was generally poverty, and sometimes sharp distress, and of this the explanation must be found in that fertile source of human woe, bad government.

If the condition of the peasantry was poor, the chief cause for this was the undue weight of taxation. The total amount raised for the needs of the government did not, perhaps, consume a larger proportion of the national income under Louis XV. than under the present French republic, but, as a result of inequalities in the imposition, the burden fell more heavily upon the lower classes than it now falls upon any class. The cost of collecting the national revenue does not now exceed five per cent.; in Louis XV.'s reign, between the profits made by the farmers to whom taxes were let and the expenses to which taxpayers were constantly subjected in the enforcement of collection, it is not perhaps an overestimate to say that the amount taken from the people exceeded by fifty per cent. the amount received by the government.[1] The change that is produced by an efficient administration was strikingly illustrated when the system of French government was reorganized under Napoleon. Six thousand competent officials did well the work which had been done ill by two hundred thousand collectors; the receipts of the government doubled, and the taxpayers were better off; a few years showed the enormous difference to the public

[1] Letrosne, *Administration des finances*, 1789, estimated that the king did not receive over one half of what the nation paid; that the gabelle took one hundred million livres from the people, and yielded only forty-five million to the government, and other taxes yielded no more in proportion.

between a vigorous and intelligent administration and
the abuses and inefficiency of the old régime.[1]

In the eighteenth century, while a large part of the
national wealth was exempt in whole or in part from
public burdens, there was no tax from which the
peasant was free; upon him fell the taille, the capi-
tation, the additional percentages for purposes of war,
and the varied impositions which together constituted
the direct taxation. So severe were they that they
often operated as a check on accumulations. Rousseau relates an incident that shows how an appearance
of squalor and need was preserved, lest the suspicion
of prosperity should invite a heavier burden of taxation. He stopped at a peasant's house and asked for
dinner. At first his host put before him only barley
bread and skimmed milk, and said this was all he had;
but, convinced at last that his visitor was not a government spy, the peasant opened his larder, produced
some ham, with good wheat bread, an omelet, and a
bottle of wine, and they dined well. He concealed
his abundance, so he told his guest, on account of the
taille, for he would be ruined by taxation if the officials did not suppose that he was dying of hunger.[2]
His fears were not ill founded, for any appearances of
well-being were sure to result in an increase of the
taille. An officer told Argenson that in the district
where he lived the taxes ought to be increased because the peasants were fatter than elsewhere; he had
seen chickens' feathers scattered about their doors,
which showed that they lived well and could pay more
to the state.[3]

[1] These changes are well summed up in Taine, *Le Régime
moderne.*
[2] *Œuvres de Rousseau,* xvi. 282.
[3] *Journal,* September, 1751.

It is probable that of every hundred francs earned by the peasant almost one half was taken for the needs of the fisc; the king's share in the crop, said Turgot, was as large as the owner's, and in addition to this were the feudal and religious imposts to which the land was subject.[1] Nominally the church took a tenth, but practically the amount collected by it was considerably less; the imposition of tithes was attended with some degree of leniency; payments were often made in kind, and it may be fairly estimated that the tithe on an average did not take more than seven per cent. of the produce of the soil.[2] It is more difficult to ascertain the amount collected by the innumerable feudal dues; while some of these were severe, many were exceedingly light, and throughout the century the old seigneurial impositions tended to fall into desuetude. Yet much more than one half of the amount earned by the peasant was used to discharge the demands made upon him by the government, the church, and the nobleman to whose feudal rights his parcel of land was subject.[3] The burden of taxation

[1] Turgot said that at Limoges, when he was superintendent, the taxes amounted to a little over one half of the product of a peasant's piece of land, but in some districts, as for instance at Saintonge, he insisted the taxes did not exceed twenty-four per cent., and on the whole he estimated the portion taken by the fisc at one third. *Avis sur l'imposition de la taille.* He probably underestimated the amount of taxation in other districts in his endeavor to obtain some alleviation for his own people.

[2] Lavergne, *Economie rurale de la France*, estimates that in 1789 the tithes did not amount to over five per cent. of the net product.

[3] Taine says over 81 per cent. of the product of a peasant's land was absorbed by imposts of all kinds, but his estimate is too high; existence could not have been supported from one fifth of the crop.

upon the French peasant under the old régime was probably over three times as heavy as it is at present, and as a result, even in times of prosperity, his lot was hard.

When the margin for subsistence was so small, it is manifest that a failure of the crop was sure to be attended by serious results. Such failures were not infrequent, and their effects were aggravated by the restraints upon the movement of grain which continued in force until late in the century. It is in these periods that we read accounts of hideous misery among large classes of men. In Paris indeed, by the constant efforts of the government, the price of bread was kept within some bounds; the capital received the same attention that Rome did under the emperors; even at large cost to the state, food was obtained for the metropolis at prices which avoided the peril of serious discontent among a swarming population.

The remote provinces received no such fatherly care when the crop was insufficient; not only were there no large charities which could relieve distress, but the restraints on the shipment of grain from more fortunate sections increased the danger of actual starvation. "More Frenchmen have died of want within two years," Argenson wrote in 1740, at a season when the crops had been deficient, "than were killed in all the wars of Louis XIV."[1] Doubtless this was a gross exaggeration, but there are many accounts which tell of the sufferings of the peasantry at such periods. Massillon writes from Auvergne, also in 1740, "The people of our country live in misery, they have neither furniture nor beds; during part of the year the most of them have no nourishment, except bread made of

---

[1] *Mém. d'Argenson*, iii. 92.

oats and barley, and even this they must snatch from their own mouths and those of their children in order to pay the taxes. . . . I see these unseemly sights every year. . . . The negroes of our islands are happier."

Even when an average crop relieved the danger of actual starvation, travelers tell us of the spectacles of misery that met them in many parts of the land. The houses of the peasantry were little better than huts, small, filthy, often without windows; the inmates were clothed in rags, barefooted, haggard, unwashed, ignorant, and miserable.

Such was not always their condition. Excessive impositions were the chief cause of the peasant's misery, and where those were lightened his lot was often one of comparative comfort. In the irregularities of the French system, while most of the peasantry were overtaxed, some escaped any excessive burden. In the southern provinces, and especially in Languedoc, they enjoyed a considerable measure of prosperity. A larger degree of local self-government, a partial exemption from the financial and commercial system in which the rest of the country was involved, secured for them an amount of well-being far exceeding that of most of the French people. "In Languedoc, Provence, and Dauphiny," writes Argenson during the worst of the famine of 1740, "there is an abundance of everything. . . . Commerce is free, and wheat is never lacking."[1] Later in the century, Arthur Young tells us of finding filth, misery, and poverty in one district, while in another the houses were neat, the peasants were well fed, and the signs of well-being were manifest. Unfortunately, in the greater part of France the condition of the peasantry was bad, the

[1] *Argenson*, November, 1740.

instances of prosperity were the exceptions and not the rule. In Berri, Young writes that he found the husbandry poor and the people miserable; we may be sure their condition was no better fifty years earlier; in Orleans, the fields were scenes of pitiable management, as the houses were scenes of extreme misery; Poitou was poor and unimproved; in Brittany, there was hideous wretchedness, he found there only privileges and poverty. "One third of what I have seen of this province," he writes, "seems uncultivated, and nearly all of it is plunged in misery." In Limousin, said Turgot, after the payment of taxes there remained not over thirty livres for each person with which to provide food and clothing and shelter. Even in relative value this sum would be less than twenty dollars now, and it seems incredible that on so beggarly a pittance life could be sustained. It is not strange that he adds, "Agriculture, as it is practiced by our peasantry, is like life in the galleys."

If starvation had been the ordinary lot of the French peasants, the race would have become extinct; on the contrary, they increased in numbers during the eighteenth century, slowly during the first half and with somewhat greater rapidity in the forty years preceding the Revolution. Notwithstanding unfair taxation and imperfect culture of the soil, as a result of laborious industry their condition improved. Walpole, traveling through France from Boulogne to Paris in 1765, writes, "I find this country wonderfully enriched since I saw it four-and-twenty years ago. Boulogne is grown quite a snug, plump town, with a number of new houses. The worst villages are tight, and wooden shoes have disappeared." Improvement, even in the early part of the century, is indicated by

another sure criterion, a rise in the price of land. Increased activity in business followed the reforms in
the currency of 1726, and an enhancement in the
value of farms seems to have attended it. In 1726,
the average price of agricultural land was estimated
at twenty-five dollars an acre; by 1750, this had risen
to thirty-five dollars.[1]

Notwithstanding the burden of taxation and the
pressure of need, the peasantry during all the century
continued to increase its holdings of the soil. Small
as were the earnings of peasant proprietors, if, by
means of the most rigorous economy, anything remained at the end of the year, it was put one side, and
the only thing that would open the box containing
their hoards was the possibility of acquiring another
bit of land. A thirst, not for gold, but for land, has
been characteristic of the French peasant as far back
as his history can be traced, and opportunities were
not wanting for new purchases. A large proportion
of the nobility were non-residents, their land yielded
them little, and ownership did not of itself bring the
social influence which had so important an effect on
the holding of land in England. The French nobleman was at court, he was in debt, and he received
small returns from his estates in the provinces. It
is evident, therefore, that it was for the interest of
the gentleman to sell, and the peasant was usually the
only purchaser. Thus, little by little, an acre here
and an acre there, the slow process of accumulation
by the peasantry went on, and it went on with as
much rapidity in the eighteenth century as at any era
of the past.

[1] These figures are derived from the reports of sales given in
Avenel, *Histoire économique*, p. 388.

CHAPTER II.

THE death of the Duke of Orleans left vacant the
position of prime minister. Louis XV. was a boy of
thirteen; though legally of age, he was not old enough
to perform the duties of his office, and the successor of
Orleans would be the actual ruler of the kingdom.
Young as Louis was, it was by his choice that the
minister must be designated, but the desires of the
sovereign were controlled by a man who had succeeded
in obtaining, to an unusual degree, his affection and
his confidence; the royal scholar listened with the
trustfulness of youth to the counsels of the preceptor,
who was to be known in history as Cardinal Fleury.
Like many of the Catholic clergy who attained prominence and power, Fleury came from humble stock.[1]
His father was a receiver of taxes, and the son gained
his education at the cost of the privations which are
the lot of needy students.[2] He chose the church as
his profession, and as a priest his conduct was deco-
rous, moral, and charitable. But he was not a man
of fervent religious character; always a reputable
priest, his interests were in the world and not in the
church.

He possessed many qualities which are of value for

---

[1] Duclos says that he belonged to an ancient and noble family,
but the pedigrees invented for those who achieve greatness are
subject to suspicion.

[2] St. Simon, ii. 148.

worldly advancement. His person was handsome, his
manners combined dignity with unfailing affability,
he was full of tact and free from greed; he made
many friends and few enemies. Such a man rarely
lacks patrons. The favor of Cardinal Bonzi obtained
for him a position as one of the queen's almoners,
and after her death he was appointed almoner of
Louis XIV.; he became an inmate of the court, and
was received as a welcome member of society. A
well-mannered abbé, who was always agreeable and
never indecorous, could reasonably expect to be made
a bishop. Louis XIV., it is said, regarded the abbé
as better fitted for life at court than for the charge
of souls, but, at the intercession of Cardinal Noailles,
Fleury was chosen as bishop of Frejus, a small and
unimportant diocese in the south of France.[1] He did
not incur the reproach of becoming a non-resident; for
sixteen years he dwelt among his flock, performing
his episcopal duties with great propriety and with
little zeal. An unimportant see might well have satisfied the ambition of a man of moderate parts and
cautious character, but Fleury retained his taste for
the court and wearied of the life of a country bishop.
In 1715, when he was past sixty, he resigned his
post, and soon afterward he was named by Louis
XIV.'s will as preceptor of Louis XV., who was
then a child of five. The position was peculiarly

[1] Madame de Maintenon, writing to Noailles in 1699, says:
"M. l'abbé de Fleury n'étoit pas lui seul un personnage à être
sitôt évêque." *Cor. gén.*, iv. 297. St. Simon, ii. 143, attributes
his promotion to the same cause, and he was usually well informed. He reports that the king said to Noailles, "I do this
with regret, and you will repent of your choice," which is quite
probable. The prophecy was verified, for in the conflict over
the Unigenitus Fleury was always opposed to Noailles.

adapted to him; he soon gained the confidence of his
pupil, and in time this made him the chief man in
France, with an authority as absolute as that of Richelieu or Mazarin.

The choice of Fleury as preceptor seems to have
been judicious, and the influence which he long possessed was on the whole wisely exercised. Fleury
was not a man to instill heroic views into his pupil's
mind, but Louis was not a man who could have im-
bibed them. The king was fairly well educated, and
the defects of his character, which made the later part
of his reign a blot on French history, could have been
corrected by no instructor.

The amiability and mildness of Fleury's character
soon aroused a warm personal affection in his pupil;
if Louis lived, it was plain that the affable preceptor
was not a person to be disregarded. He manifested,
however, little desire for advancement; he had led a
tranquil life, and it did not seem probable that when
approaching seventy he would develop a lust for
power or place. Although he seemed unambitious,
yet he realized the advantages of his position, and was
allured by no dignity which would interfere with his
personal relations with the king. In 1721, the Duke
of Orleans offered him the archbishopric of Rheims.
This was among the great prizes of the French church;
the Archbishop of Rheims was one of the ecclesiasti-
cal peers of the realm; by him the king was conse-
crated; he enjoyed the income of a farmer general
and the dignity of a prince. Yet no solicitation could
induce Fleury to accept a position which might loosen
his hold upon his pupil's affections. His friends suggested that he should confide the duties of the office
to a vicar and content himself with receiving its rev-

enues, but Fleury was not greedy for money, and he knew the advantages of a reputation for propriety of conduct; more sincerely than is common he persisted in declaring, "Nolo episcopari." [1] When he was living in his former diocese, it is said that he once signed a letter, "Fleury, by divine wrath, bishop of Frejus." [2] It is certain that he had lost his taste for bishoprics.

The sudden death of the Duke of Orleans left the way open for Fleury; he had but to say the word and be declared the prime minister of France. He was now a man of seventy, and at that age few are willing to postpone the gratification of their ambition to an indefinite future. Whether from timidity or from hesitation, the word was not spoken.

If Fleury was uncertain, there was an aspirant who never hesitated to ask for what he wanted. The Duke of Bourbon was the head of the great House of Condé, and he inherited qualities which that family had often displayed since they deserted the faith and the heroic practices of their ancestors a century before. The duke combined the greed of his grandfather with the violent ambition of his great-grandfather; though he was a young man during the regency of Orleans, he had been persistent, and successful in demanding office and favor. He reaped fabulous gains from the operations of Law; he asked enormous advantages in return for the protection he extended, and the unfortunate adventurer was not in position to say no to so powerful a nobleman. It was reported that Bourbon had carried off many millions in gold

---

[1] *Mém. de St. Simon*, xvii. 274–280.

[2] This is stated by Voltaire, but like most historical anecdotes, it is probably incorrect.

from the spoils of Law's bank and the Mississippi Company; the government compelled some humbler speculators to disgorge their gains, but no one ventured to disturb the head of the House of Condé.

It was in the evening of December 2, 1723, that Orleans was suddenly stricken with apoplexy. The Duke of Bourbon was then at Versailles; the moment he heard the news he waited upon the king, and demanded the position of prime minister. Whether Fleury was too modest to ask this great office for himself, or whether he feared to offend a man of Bourbon's rank and violent character, he at once declared that his majesty could do no better than charge the duke with the burden of his affairs. The young king turned to his preceptor and nodded his head, without saying a word, and thus the appointment was made.[1]

The Duke of Bourbon was thirty-one years of age when he became prime minister. Few men were less fitted for the duties of such a place; he was without political capacity or political experience, and his brief ministry was characterized by corruption, bad judgment, and bigotry. The only principles which actuated him on assuming office were a strong resolve to get what he could for himself, and an equally strong resolve that the family of Orleans should get nothing. The duke had a fanatical hatred for any one who bore the name of Orleans; the regent had tried to satisfy in some degree the incessant and insatiable demands of his cousin, but the effort was not successful; much as Bourbon had received, he always wanted more.

[1] St. Simon, xix. 201, 202. St. Simon says that Fleury had agreed to recommend Bourbon for prime minister if Orleans died.

Now that he was himself in power, the fact that any measure had obtained the regent's approval made his successor desirous for its repeal, and he was haunted by a constant fear lest the new Duke of Orleans should obtain greater prominence than himself in the councils of the king. There was little reason to be disquieted on this score. The regent's son possessed neither the vices nor the virtues of his father, and he had inherited none of his abilities. Beginning life amid the dissipation of the Palais Royal, he ended his days amid the austerities of the abbey of Sainte Genevieve, but he was so unfortunately constituted that in him even virtue became grotesque; the son of the regent and the grandfather of Philippe Egalité proved the uncertainty of heredity by giving his time to writing treatises against the theatre, in the intervals of studies on the theological works of Theodore of Mopsuestia; although his income exceeded three million francs, he slept on a straw pallet, fasted with severity, went without fires on cold winter days, and made his fellow monks miserable by the rigorous discipline on which he insisted. Such practices killed him at exactly the same age that debauchery closed the career of his father.[1] Bourbon was not a man of ability, but he had little trouble in pushing his pious cousin out of his path.

The duke was controlled by another passion stronger even than his jealousy of Orleans, and that was his affection for Mme. de Prie. She was a woman well fitted to please; her conversation was witty and agreeable; she had read much; her memory was tenacious; her beauty was set off by a charming air of modesty and reserve. Never were appearances more deceptive: no

---

[1] *Journal de Barbier*, v. 156 *et pas.*; *Mém. d'Argenson*, iii. 402.

woman regarded virtue less; she was violent in her
hates; she was selfish and greedy and false. "The
Duke of Bourbon's mistress," wrote Bolingbroke, "is
attached to him by no inclination, and is at once the
most corrupt and ambitious jade alive."[1]

Hardly had the duke assumed his office, when the
attention of the community was attracted by a new
vagary of the Bourbon prince, to place whom on the
Spanish throne Louis XIV. involved France in years
of war. Superstition constantly gained a stronger
hold on the cloudy and enfeebled mind of Philip V.,
and now he suddenly announced his intention to abdicate. This scheme had long been in his mind.[2] It
was not strange that Philip himself should desire a
life of religious retirement, in the belief that thereby
he could increase his chance for salvation, but his
wife was an ambitious woman, who cared for temporal
as well as spiritual kingdoms. She had long ruled
her husband with an authority divided only with his
confessor, and she had no taste for abdications; but
increasing fear of hell so absorbed Philip's mind that
at last Elizabeth's influence could no longer prevail
against it.[3] In 1720, he succeeded in having her join
him in a written promise that they would both retire
from the world by All Saints' Day, 1723. Doubtless
the queen thought that if she could postpone the evil
day for three years, events would arise to change the
king's mind, but she underestimated his tenacity of
purpose. To prepare for his retirement he built the

---

[1] Letter of January 12, 1724.

[2] "Every day," wrote an ambassador, "he has been growing
more mistrustful, more timorous, and more scrupulous." *Aff.
Etr.*, 330, 289.

[3] *Ib., pas.*

magnificent palace of San Ildefonso, at the little village of Balsaim, near the gloomy Escurial of Philip II., and there he sought to surround himself with a splendor which should remind him of the glories of Versailles. His retreat was somewhat delayed, probably at his wife's solicitations, but at last he would delay no longer. In January, 1724, Philip surprised his council by announcing that, after years of reflection on the miseries of life, he had resolved to abdicate his throne in order to devote himself to the service of God and labor at the great work of his own salvation.[1] He addressed a letter to his son, bidding him to govern wisely, to cultivate a special devotion for the Holy Virgin, and to sustain the tribunal of the Inquisition, that rampart of the faith which had preserved the purity of religion in Spain and saved her from the heresies which ravaged other lands.[2] Having thus displayed the measure of his statesmanship, this infirm representative of the Bourbon family retired to seclusion amid the beauties of San Ildefonso, there to make his salvation sure.[3]

He was succeeded by his son Louis, a prince who showed no signs of possessing any greater measure of ability than his father. His reign was brief, and seven months after his father's abdication the young

---

[1] *Archives d'Alcala.*

[2] *Ib.*

[3] Coxe, in his *Spain under the Bourbons*, advanced the theory that Philip's abdication was intended to make it easier for him to succeed to the French throne, in the not improbable event of Louis XV.'s death. This theory cannot be adopted in view of the documents which are now open to examination. Philip always intended to claim the French throne if his nephew died, but his abdication was due to the morbid piety of a weak mind, and not to the counsels of ambition.

king was carried off by smallpox. A younger brother should now have succeeded to the throne, but
Elizabeth was resolved that she would no longer be
kept from the enjoyment of power by the sickly piety
of her husband. Philip himself seems to have wearied of a life of retirement, and was not averse to
resuming the crown, but he was now involved in new
fears. He had promised God to abdicate; could he
leave his retreat and return to the world without
incurring fresh danger of perdition? His confessor
was consulted and, to the dismay of Elizabeth, he decided that the king would be guilty of grievous sin if
he violated his promise. "You are a rascal," cried
the Italian nurse, who was a great personage in this
strange royal family, to the confessor who had thus
interfered with the queen's projects. "I would do
the king good service if I ran a dagger in you." The
French still fancied that it was for their interest to
keep the grandson of Louis XIV. on the throne, and
Marshal Tessé sought to counteract the effect produced on the king by the scruples of the confessor.
At first he was unsuccessful. "I don't want to be
damned," said Philip to the marshal; "they may do
what they please with my kingdom, but I am going
to save my soul." [1] The queen now conceived the
happy device of consulting the papal nuncio. More
worldly wise than the confessor, he advised Philip
that he could resume the crown and incur no risk of
hell fire, and the monarch allowed himself to be per-
suaded. For twenty-two years more he remained on
the Spanish throne, but he still clung to the idea of
abdication; at times his hypochondriacal fancies were
especially strong, and in his efforts to carry his pur-

[1] For all this, see correspondence of Tessé, *Aff. Etr.*, 1724.

pose into effect he showed the cunning which is often found in persons of infirm mind. On one occasion when the queen had left him for a moment, he hastily signed a new abdication, and had it conveyed surreptitiously from his room. She learned of this, and succeeded in recapturing the fatal paper before it was too late. At last she induced her husband to take an oath that he would sign no more abdications; when at times he was especially fearful of incurring damnation by remaining a king, she could threaten him with the same danger if he violated his oath. By such devices he was kept on the throne until his death, but it was Elizabeth of Parma, and not Philip of France, who controlled the destinies of Spain.

Bourbon had been anxious that Philip should return to the throne, but actuated by his own ambition, or by the disappointed vanity of his mistress, the duke now decided on a step which caused Spain to abandon the alliance of France for that of Austria.

In 1721, it had been agreed that Louis XV. should marry his kinswoman, the Spanish infanta, and a daughter of Philip V. She was then a child of three, but she was sent to Paris with much parade, there to receive a French education, and await the proper age for the solemnization of the nuptials. Three years had passed since then; to violate this agreement and send the princess back to her parents was to affront them in the sight of all Europe, and to incur the utmost ill will of the Spanish king; but the Duke of Bourbon decided upon this step for reasons personal to himself. The infanta was only six years old, and a long time must still elapse before the marriage could be consummated; should Louis die, leaving no son, the heir to the throne, as by law

established, was the Duke of Orleans, the person whom
Bourbon most envied and hated.   Moreover the Spanish alliance had been a measure of the regent; the
future queen would not owe her elevation to Bourbon, and Spain would have no interest in his retention
of office.   He wished to choose a wife for the king
upon whose gratitude he could rely; a queen with an
amiable character, a pliant disposition, and a grateful
heart would insure a continuance of favor to the duke
and his mistress.

He accordingly laid before the council the dangers
which France might incur if Louis remained unmar-
ried, and advised the immediate choice of a bride of
mature years.   No one ventured to oppose the wish
of the prime minister.   Fleury contented himself with
a mild opposition, and the young king, who was not
yet fifteen, was perfectly indifferent on the subject.
The infanta was returned to Spain, and her father
was informed that the desire of all good Frenchmen
for a dauphin with all possible haste compelled Louis
to select another person for his wife.   Diplomatic relations between the countries were broken off, but
Philip did not allow his pique to lead him to any
more violent measures.[1]

It was easy to find some one willing to be queen
of France, and Louis was ready to accept any one
suggested by his advisers, but Bourbon and Mme. de

[1] The Duke of Bourbon asked Philip to make the husband
of Mme. de Prie a grandee, a title which would have descended
to a child Bourbon had by her. (See his letter to Tessé.) If
this request had been granted, the infanta would probably not
have been sent away. " 'This one-eyed scoundrel,' said Philip's
wife, with her usual vigor, ' has sent back our daughter because
the king would not create the husband of his harlot a grandee
of Spain.' " Letter of Stanhope.

Prie were more difficult to please. A list was prepared, upon which appeared the names of one hundred princesses, with a statement of their physical, mental, and moral qualities.[1] Bourbon summarily ran his pen through eighty-three of the names, as out of the question, and among those rejected was the one who finally obtained the prize. Of the seventeen that were deemed worthy of discussion, the most eligible was the Princess Elizabeth of Russia, the daughter of Peter the Great and the future empress of that country. Her mother, Catherine I., undismayed by the prospect of ninety-nine competitors, declared that in personal charms and in the political advantages which she could offer, her daughter outranked them all. In part, certainly, her opinion was correct. Russian princesses did not yet stand on the same footing with those of Austria or Spain; the marriage of one of them with the king of France would have signalized the reception of Russia among the civilized states of the west, and the choice of Elizabeth would have secured for France the active support of her country during half a century. Catherine offered to make a treaty of alliance, offensive and defensive, and to exert the influence of Russia for the choice of a French prince as king of Poland, if her daughter could become queen of France. The French ambassador at St. Petersburg urged the wisdom of this choice, not only on political, but on personal grounds. "In Russia," he wrote, "it is an established maxim, that all women, from princesses to bourgeoises, have a blind submission to the wishes of their husbands."[2]

[1] *Aff. Etr. Fr.*, 314.
[2] Letter of Campredon, April 13, 1725. All the correspondence in reference to the proposed Russian alliance is found in

But this match was not to Bourbon's taste, and he gave little heed to the advantages it might bring to France, if it would not advance his own interests. The low birth of the mother of the Princess Elizabeth, he wrote, must be regarded as an obstacle to her choice, and instead of her, he recommended one of his own sisters. As to one of them, the brother admitted that something might be said against her figure, but the other combined virtue, wisdom, and grace.[1] Notwithstanding her attractions, this alliance met with opposition. Fleury was not in favor of it.[2] It is probable also that Mme. de Prie saw no advantage to herself in making a queen of Bourbon's sister, and the voice of his mistress overcame his fraternal zeal. The plan was abandoned, and the throne of France was offered to a daughter of George I., if she would consent to become a Catholic.[3] If George had been simply Elector of Hanover, such a condition would have met with no opposition. Even when the choice of a faith was not postponed until the choice of a husband, the religion of a daughter of a German prince was rarely allowed to stand in the way of her advancement. But George was on the throne of England as the representative of Protestantism. All that kept the Stuart pretender in exile was his Catholicism; if the English people had not regarded the Roman church with fear and aversion, an ignorant and licentious Hanoverian prince would not have been

his letters at the *Aff. Etr., Cor. de Russie.* The subject is well treated by Vandal, *Louis XV. et Elisabeth de Russie.*

[1] Rapport du duc de Bourbon au roi, *Aff. Etr. Fr.*, 314.

[2] *Procès verbal, Arch. Nat.;* Walpole to Newcastle, March 13, 1725.

[3] *Aff. Etr. Angleterre*, 1725, 350.

Lightning Source UK Ltd.
Milton Keynes UK
UKHW040918281119
354396UK00006B/710/P

9 781377 875903